Antonio Evaristo Morales-Pita, PhD is a retired professor of international political economy at DePaul University in Chicago, who had taught for fifty-four years in Cuban, Mexican, and American universities. He has been recipient of eight international awards as a professor, and a scholar in the three aforementioned countries.

He has published eight books, six of them as a scholar in mathematics, economics, research and environment in Cuba and Mexico, and the remaining two as non-fiction, epic, and historical biographies in the United States. He is a polyglot traveler of the world.

06/26/21

To: ~~[scribbled out]~~

In memoriam to my mother, Siria,
who was my role model in education and my first source
of inspiration.

To my wife, Gladys,
whose love is my constant inspiration to get ahead in life,
and who stays alive in my thoughts and my heart.

To my two children, Rosita and Tonito,
who have been inspired by me; and I have been inspired
by them.

To my students in Cuba, Mexico, and the United States,
who have inspired me to fulfill my vocation as an
educator.

To my spiritual guardian, Father Edgar Morales,
who inspires me as a man of genuine and steadfast faith in
the Lord.

*With best wishes*

*A. Morales*

# Antonio Evaristo Morales-Pita, PhD

# Is It Possible to Inspire Anyone?

AUSTIN MACAULEY PUBLISHERS™

LONDON · CAMBRIDGE · NEW YORK · SHARJAH

**Ordering Information**
Quantity sales: Special discounts are available on quantity purchases by corporations, associations, and others. For details, contact the publisher at the address below.

**Publisher's Cataloging-in-Publication data**
Morales-Pita, PhD, Antonio Evaristo
Is It Possible to Inspire Anyone?

ISBN 9781647503963 (Paperback)
ISBN 9781647503970 (Hardback)
ISBN 9781647503987 (ePub e-book)

Library of Congress Control Number: 2021910518

www.austinmacauley.com/us

First Published (2021)
Austin Macauley Publishers LLC
40 Wall Street, 33rd Floor, Suite 3302
New York, NY 10005
USA

mail-usa@austinmacauley.com
+1 (646) 5125767

Dr. Miles Harvey, who is my inspiration in pursuing the objective of publishing a book with a serious and prestigious publishing company.

# Table of Contents

**Introduction**                                                    **11**

**First Part: What Is Inspiration and How It Can Be
        Instilled in Someone?**                              **27**

*Chapter I: What Does It Take to Be an Inspirational
        Human Being?*                                         *29*

*Chapter II: The Process of Being Inspired*              *42*

**Second Part: Examples of Inspiration in the
        Classroom and at Home**                        **67**

*Chapter III: How to Inspire Students to Accomplish
        Their Educational Goals?*                           *69*

*Chapter IV: How to Inspire Parents to Become Role
        Models in Education for
        Their Children?*                                            *77*

*Chapter V: How to Inspire Anybody to Overcome a
        Challenge?*                                               *87*

*Chapter VI: A Groundbreaking Inspirational Story*   *94*

# Introduction

*"We all have ability. The difference is how we use it."*

– Stevie Wonder, singer and songwriter

The main topic of this book can be summarized in one word 'inspiration.' This morning, August 5, 2010, on my way to the gym, I felt inspired by an unprecedented event reported on page three of the *Red Eye* newspaper. An appealing heading caught my attention: 'The Giving Spree.' There was Bill Gates's smiling face at a groundbreaking site with the following statement from him and his wife, Melinda: "We have been blessed with good fortune beyond our wildest expectations, and we are profoundly grateful. But just as these gifts are great, so we feel a great responsibility to use them well. That is why we are so pleased to join in making an explicit commitment to the Giving Pledge." I must say that I got emotional to see this gratitude and kindness instead of shocking news about crime, tyranny, and war, which are very often found in the media.

I felt inspired by this altruistic and philanthropic initiative led by successful people who represent the wealthiest part of our society. What I liked most was their sense of responsibility to use the gifts they have received from life – or from God as I see it. The attitude of this selected group of the world's billionaires is highly commendable not only because of what it represents from a human standpoint but also because the sums of money they have given will be invested in education. How many gifted minds can be saved for humanity by this group of successful human beings! Their contribution can be measured not only in terms of money but also by the time they have dedicated to helping others in need. What an inspiring event!

Many of my friends, students, acquaintances, and the readers of my book *Havana-Mérida-Chicago (A Journey to Freedom)* have openly told me – without being asked – that I have inspired them in one way or another. They said this to me spontaneously; it appeared as though they had to tell me. Was I always an inspirational person? Well, I think my mother nurtured my desire to excel in academia, and she instilled in me the need to learn, to learn relentlessly and eagerly. Maybe what struck me the most from my childhood was that she herself did not know how to read and write but felt admiration for people who were able to finish academic careers. I believe she was somewhat frustrated because her childhood was spent in a humble environment and she did not have the opportunity to study. She wanted all her children to go to school to achieve a better life.

My passion for studying led me to love teaching – I discovered that teaching somebody else was the best way to learn. I wanted to get my point across. I loved to see comprehension on the faces of my students, and I learned to read their eyes to see whether they were following me.

The first time I delivered a speech I had just turned 15. I was learning English in an economic geography course at the high school associated with the Havana Business University. As part of the course, we had to prepare a report on a state or states in the United States of America. I chose Virginia and West Virginia. Every student prepared a short paper about the state or states assigned to the student and delivered a speech about it in front of the class. Afterward, the other students were supposed to ask the speaker questions related to his or her imaginary trip to the state. I was scheduled to speak the second day the speeches were being delivered.

I found the first day of speeches to be boring, especially because of the questions my peers asked the student who gave the talk. Their questions did not elicit any further information about the state. I was fed up with questions such as how much did the trip cost? Was the weather nice during your stay? Good Lord, I had expected to learn from the questions of my peers, and I took it for granted that they had done their homework, so I raised my hand and asked a simple question to the student who had spoken about Massachusetts. I simply asked him, "Why is Boston such an important city for Massachusetts?" The student was mute; he stammered, became pale, and could not answer. I couldn't imagine that he would not know that Boston was the capital of Massachusetts. The rest of my peers stared at me, frowning, and making indecent signs with their fingers. I knew the worst was coming for me the following day.

The class session took place in the morning. The day before, I spent the whole afternoon in the library, consulting several books and encyclopedias to learn as much as possible about my two states. I was inspired to study very hard because I did not want to look foolish in front of my classmates and the instructor. I finished my studying late in the evening when the librarian closed the library.

The following morning, I spoke about the two states without any apprehension. I had done my best to prepare for the presentation and to do a good job. I couldn't ask anything else of myself. So there I was... I realized my audience would be my fellow students and that I would be explaining the subject matter to them. After I finished, I received five very hard questions. To my surprise and to that of my peers, I answered all of them exhaustively even though they would not have been answerable by a tourist briefly visiting Virginia and West Virginia. What surprised me most was that after the last answer, the whole student body stood up and gave me a round of applause. I will never forget that this event took place on April 16, 1956, shortly before I finished the Havana Business University High School. At the time I was not aware that I was inspired to give a good presentation out of my desire not to be made fun of (at the time I was still stammering and many people made fun of my poor oral articulation). Another important factor – which I could not have identified in those moments of my first academic accomplishment – was that my dedication and commitment to learning had inspired and won over the peers who had initially been against me. I was able to get my message across in an unfavorable environment. April 16, 1956, was definitely the most unforgettable day of my teenage years – it was the day my future vocation as an educator materialized 'out of thin air.'

In my book *Havana-Mérida-Chicago (A Journey to Freedom)*, readers can learn how I started to teach as a non-graduate instructor of operational research in 1967, how I created economic research teams to study agro-industrial production in Cuba and Mexico in 1982 and 1993, and, finally, how I started to work as an adjunct faculty member at DePaul University in Chicago. During this entire period, I was getting feedback both from my students and the professionals doing research under my mentorship. I was inspiring them to succeed academically. My ability to facilitate brainstorming, which I learned while leading the research team at the University of Havana and continued to develop during my unforgettable years in Mexico, made me aware that I do have inspirational skills.

After almost 30 years of intensive academic activity, I finally discovered that I could, in fact, inspire people to achieve goals in life. Delving deeply into my life, I must say that this awareness stemmed from self-publishing *Havana-Mérida-Chicago*, meeting my readers, and getting feedback from them. So, some years went by, and now I have decided to discuss the process of being inspirational by writing another book. People are often moved by reading inspirational books, papers, letters, and even notes. I will examine the inspirational process in this book.

The interaction between a human being and his or her work is an interesting phenomenon. The person has an idea that becomes concrete in an objective piece of work, so the person is transforming the world around him or herself, giving it a new form. But while a person is creating something new, that something is transforming the person by contributing to his or her skill development and experience.

By the same token, when an author writes a book, he is shaping his thoughts, ideas, and experiences, putting them in order, drawing interrelationships among them, and organizing them into a cohesive framework. Before arriving in this country in 1996, I had written six books related to my academic work in economics, mathematics, and the environment. But my experience of reaching freedom at age 55 – after having lived in four countries and the unique way in which events unfolded with God's help – led me to write my first personal book, an autobiography: *Havana-Merida-Chicago (A Journey to Freedom)*.

I wrote the book in two weeks while seated in a wheelchair in front of a computer. I had had an operation on my right ankle and was recovering at home. During those two weeks, my mind went back to my childhood, my youth, and my early days as an instructor at the University of Havana. I also looked back at my love life, my dreams of being useful to Cuba, my disillusionment with the Communist Revolution led by Fidel Castro, my unforgettable time of rebirth as a teacher and scientific leader in Mexico, and my wonderful journey to the United States. While I was writing the book, I was being transformed by the understanding of how great an impact God has had on my life, how important my mother's fostering my love for education had been, and how blessed I was to have a wife like Gladys who was able – and still is despite her physical disappearance – to give me so much peace, pure love, and happiness. At the same time, as I was writing and reviewing the pages of the book, I was being transformed into a better human being. But this was just the beginning.

After the manuscript was written, two years went by without it being accepted by a literary agent or a recognized publisher, so I had to self-publish the book. As I write this manuscript, I remembered having been able to sell 2,333 copies of the book on my own without the help of any literary agent or publisher and without the book being stocked in any bookstore. I tried many times to contact literary agents and publishers, but my efforts were unsuccessful.

So how was I able to do it? First of all, because I was convinced that the book was good, I was ready to go 'through thick and thin' to make it available to readers. I knew I was filling a void in the available literature about immigrants escaping from communism and rebuilding their lives. I was guided by a sincere calling to broaden the horizons of the reading public, regardless of its nationality. It was also an example of a 55-year-old man who started again from scratch – after several attempts in Cuba and Mexico – and was able to establish himself successfully in this country.

When somebody is persuaded to achieve a goal, he or she always finds a rationale to make decisions and to undertake a course of action. So I started to offer talks and book signings at colleges, universities, book fairs, churches, social events, and even in my gym. I traveled outside Chicago to nearby Aurora and more distant Miami, Los Angeles, Houston, and Pittsburgh among other cities. With God's help, I was contracted by the Resource Center for Bilingual Parents of the Chicago Public Schools to offer talks to parents about the necessity of becoming role models in their children's education. At these gatherings, I could also promote my book.

The work was hard, especially at the book fairs, but I was quite successful and was able to sell approximately 25 copies during eight consecutive hours. In order to sell 25 copies, I had to talk to approximately 50 or 60 prospective buyers. At the end of the day, I was exhausted and almost hoarse. On many occasions – after a five or ten-minute talk with a prospective buyer – he or she told me, "Thanks for the information. Your life story is interesting. I don't have cash with me right now, but I will return soon." Oftentimes that person never returned, but immediately afterward, I was already approaching somebody else with my eyes full of hope and a smile on my face.

I also reaped many huge rewards. I spent three wonderful months going to Aurora at least twice a week to promote my book with the help of a great Mexican friend who was committed to helping Aurora children rebuild their lives through education and self-improvement. The first talk I offered in Aurora was in a school for children coming from broken homes or displaying unacceptable social behavior. In that talk, I emphasized the joy of making money on the basis of honest and hard work and the satisfaction of feeling useful to society and receiving a reward for that work. At the end of the talk, I summarized the book. Some students were paying attention, others were looking at the ceiling, and others were talking to their peers. In the audience, one boy stood out. He was asking questions. His attention was fixed on the talk. He happened to be seated just beside the exit door, and when I was about to leave the classroom, I told him, "You will make it. You will succeed." On my next visit to Aurora, my Mexican friend commented that my talk had impressed some students, especially the one whom I had approached. The boy wanted to buy the book. In future visits to Aurora, I tried to find him to give him the book as a gift, but I was unable to.

18 months later, I was selling my book at a book fair in Cicero. On the first day, I observed a young man standing close to the table, listening to my promotion with prospective customers. He was almost a child, and his face was somewhat familiar to me, but I could not remember where I had seen him.

All of the sudden, he addressed me and said, "I want to buy the book." I smiled at him, saying that I was glad to hear that, but I thought that he might not be able to afford its price. He said he only had three dollars. He then looked at me and said, "I want to buy the book and I will get the money. I will come back before you leave." After some hours went by, the boy returned and started to take money out of his pockets. He placed one five-dollar bill, several singles, and some quarters, dimes, and nickels on my desk.

I was impressed by this attitude. I had never seen anybody so intent on buying the book. I told him, "Stop it. That is enough. The book will be yours regardless of how much money you have." He answered "I want to buy the book at its price. Please, count the money." He had been able to gather $14.65. I embraced him and autographed and dedicated the book to him. He had tears in his eyes, and, of course, there were tears in mine as well. The young man took the book in his hands, kissed it, and went away. I was in shock because I was still beating my brains out trying to remember where I had seen my best customer. Shortly before arriving home, I remembered. He was the boy from

Aurora. I didn't even know his name, but I knew he was inspired by my talk.

In a nutshell, my direct work with my 2,333 readers enabled me to know what each of them liked about the book. I knew what a varied assortment of readers including men, women, students, immigrants, native-born Americans, parents, teachers, and Hispanic community leaders liked about the book.

In other words, the book transformed my life. I became more interested in the Hispanic community. I started to write about political and social issues in newspapers. I appeared on T.V. programs, talking about the book, the Cuban economy, the American economy, and so on. I was even recognized by the DePaul University Office for Relations with the Media by receiving the Media Star Award in 2008.

A man creates a book, and the book transforms the man. But my transformation went on and on. The talks with the parents of Chicago Public School children and the testimonies of my readers made me aware of one special characteristic of my personality – I am an inspiring human being. Good gracious, I had become an inspirational speaker!

Rereading my book *Havana-Merida-Chicago* against the comments of my readers, I could gather that inspiration is present in every chapter, on every page of the book. The inspiration stems from the fact that I never gave up, I never felt defeated, and I always found a way to overcome the immense obstacles encountered in my journey to freedom. The inspiration also comes from the fact that – after overcoming quagmires and obstacles – I was able to succeed. I highly encourage the readers of this book to go to the website for my book, www.gladysantonio.com, and read the testimonies of my readers. They are impressive, moving, and inspirational in themselves.

My conversion to Jesus Christ, explained in Chapter IV of *Havana-Merida-Chicago*, showed me the powerful impact of God on my life and allowed me to understand how apparent strokes of luck were the results of the wonderfully articulated plan of a Superior Being. I would like to reiterate that I believe that one of the most important outcomes of having self-published *Havana-Merida-Chicago* is that I became aware of my gift to inspire people. If the Lord gave me that precious gift, it is my duty to use it for the benefit of mankind, and that is why I am writing this book. I have to share with my readers the experience of being inspirational and being inspired.

This book does not provide specific tactics and strategies of inspiration for each and every situation. It is a book about inspiring anyone in any situation, from learning a general skill to applying it and being tenacious in its application until one's goal is attained.

It is very much like studying with the purpose of learning. The highest-level course taken in the most prestigious university in the world and taught by the most experienced and pedagogically competent educator cannot claim to teach everything about a particular subject. No theory can ever anticipate all the particular situations of real life. The task of the best educator is to provide students with the skills that will allow them to solve on their own the complex problems in the real world. The student should not expect to find the same example that the instructor explained to him. This is why, in my lectures, I emphasize developing a student's reasoning skills and not a student's memory. This book is written by an inborn educator whose mission in life has been to develop analytic and cognitive skills in his students so that they will be able to become top-quality professionals. Therefore, I teach the theory – which I have developed through my practice and experience – and present some cases of inspiration that I have personally encountered. It is up to the reader to apply this theory successfully with an optimistic attitude, believing in himself or herself.

The book contains seven chapters preceded by an introduction and a test to be taken before reading the first chapter and again after finishing the book. The book is divided into three parts.

The first part – 'What Is Inspiration and How Can It Be Instilled in Someone?' – I teach the theory – which I have developed through my practice and experience – and I present some cases of inspiration that I have personally encountered. It is up to the reader to apply this theory successfully with an optimistic attitude, believing in himself or herself.

The first part – 'What Is Inspiration and How Can It Be Instilled in Someone?' – includes two chapters.

Chapter I – 'What Does It Take to Be an Inspirational Person?'

This chapter contains a general description of the people who have truly inspired me and the reasons why they exerted such influence on me. After profiling these inspirational people, I analyze the features they all have in common and draw some preliminary conclusions before passing to the second part of the chapter, which is dedicated to the person to be inspired.

After discussing some of the psychological characteristics of the person to be inspired, I generalize about the person's disposition and then relate it to the psychology of the inspirer. An important conclusion is that the inspirational process must have two sides which, in fact, complement one another.

Some *Food for Thought* questions are included at the end of the chapter.

Chapter II – 'What Is the Process of Being Inspired and How Does It Take Place?'

The chapter begins with a discussion of the ways in which I was inspired as a professor, the main challenges I had to face, and how I overcame all of those challenges. The motivation for inspiring another person as well as inspirational methods are clearly elaborated in this context. Then, I transcribe the testimonies of seven different students who have been inspired in diverse ways – from enrolling in more than one course to finishing a bachelor's degree, from being accepted by the University of Chicago to holding a job, and starting a Master's of Science program abroad. Finally, the chapter contains an example of someone who never was my student but was inspired by my book *Havana-Merida-Chicago* without having previously met me.

The last part of Chapter II concludes with my experiences as an inspired student, the challenges I had to overcome, and the motivation I found in myself to meet them.

The second part of the book – 'Examples of Inspiration in the Classroom and at Home' – includes two chapters: Chapter III – 'How to Inspire Students to Achieve Their Educational Goals,' and Chapter IV – 'How to Inspire Parents to Become Role Models for Their Children in Their Education.' Each of these chapters has the same structure. On the basis of my personal experience as a professor and as an academic and research team leader, I explain the conditions required to be an inspirational educator, an inspirational parent, and an inspirational leader.

Chapters III and IV can be used to supplement textbooks because they relate to the conditions of being an inspirational instructor and an inspired student. The last section of each of these two chapters consists of essay-type questions for the readers to self-evaluate their development and potential in each area.

The third part of the book – 'The Inspiration to Face and to Overcome a Challenge' – includes two chapters. Chapter V – 'How to Inspire Anybody to Overcome a Challenge' – discusses the inspirational process from a strictly human point of view. This chapter shows the interrelationship between the motivation, courage, and tenacity required to instill inspiration in students. It is deeper than the chapters that lead up to it. Here, I discuss how instructors can develop students' cognitive skills by relating their own experiences as students and educators and how the results obtained in different students – when they are confronted with the inspirational experience – will vary. Another important part of this chapter relates to the inspiration that

Siria Pita, my deceased mother, was able to instill not only in her children but also in her friends despite her extremely limited education. Her passion for education is a good lesson for parents. They should thoroughly study the innumerable ways she motivated her children and the outstanding results she was able to obtain.

At the end of the chapter, the readers are asked questions for them to meditate. About two challenges they have faced, one that had a positive result and another that had an unsatisfactory outcome.

Chapter VI – 'A Profound Inspirational Experience.' The introduction to this last chapter describes the essence of inspiration from the perspective of a professor. This chapter, however, is largely written from the viewpoint of a student who has been extraordinarily motivated to be inspired. It deals with a long-term inspirational experience as recounted by that exceptional student. I asked him to write this part, and he did so in a splendid manner, showing the sequence of inspirational events that formidably modified his career. This is an interesting case of mutual inspiration between a professor and a student.

As an introduction to getting deeper into the essence of this book, may I suggest the readers to think about the following questions related to inspirational issues?

**Food for Thought**

Please, meditate about these two questions:

1. Do you believe to be an inspirational person?
2. Can you be inspired by someone else?

# First Part

# What Is Inspiration and How It Can Be Instilled in Someone?

# Chapter I
# What Does It Take to Be an Inspirational Human Being?

*"It is not the will to win, but the will to prepare to win that makes the difference."*

– Paul 'Bear' Bryant

Today it is August 29, 2009. As I write these lines, I am watching a posthumous ceremony honoring Ted Kennedy. I am looking at the very special funeral of somebody who was never the president of the United States yet is nonetheless receiving a funeral worthy of a president. Ted Kennedy was and is an inspiration for bipartisanship. He was able to get along well with and befriend both Democrats and Republicans despite their political differences. His inspirational personality was so strong that it could overcome the rancor, animosity, and resentment that frequently stem from political disagreements, especially at the congressional level. Ted Kennedy was and is an inspiration as a politician. He was somebody who in fact placed the interests of the country above partisan interests. May this book pay a modest homage to this great American!

I have met several people who inspired me to be a better person. In the chronological order they appeared in my life, I will mention them and how they inspired me.

Siria Pita, my beloved mother, was born to a poor family. Her parents could not afford the tuition and books even for primary school, but she always loved to study. She was illiterate until she turned 51 and was only able to finish high school at age 81, yet she was a constant presence in her children's schools. She could not help any of her children with their schoolwork, but she always showed respect and support for their studies. She became the role model for her four children in their education. All of her children finished college. I owe it to her that I learned English when I was 14 years old. I owe to her the punctuality with which I attend to whatever activity I participate in. I owe to her the pride I take in doing good work responsibly and to the best of my ability. I owe to her my tenacious attitude. Although she passed away in 1998, she continues being my inspiration and role model, and the thought of her comes to my mind whenever I face an obstacle. Siria Pita would not like me to give up. She never did.

Florentino Morales, my beloved father, worked as a stevedore at the Havana Central Produce Market for 40 years without a single absence or instance of tardiness. A man who never smoked and drank only on very special occasions, he was always attentive to his family's welfare. I owe to my father my sense of discipline and commitment to work and my desire to always meet deadlines in advance. I owe to my father my abstinence from smoking and drinking to excess and my very healthy eating habits. Although he passed away in 1978, he has remained my inspiration as a responsible father, especially when I had to divorce the mother of my children and to endure conflict with her. It was clear to me that the divorce took place with their mother and not with my children.

Aníbal Roger, my mathematics teacher in high school, showed me what a good educator was about. He was patient; he cared about his students. His pedagogical objective was to be understood, not to show off his knowledge, and he wanted to get his message across to everyone in the class – from the best student to the one who was struggling to pass. He showed me the importance of applying knowledge acquired in the classroom to real life. Although he passed away some years ago, he remains my inspiration as an educator. His patience and self-control are unforgettable.

Rosa Morales Pacheco and Antonio Morales Pacheco, my two children, my two only children. They inspire me as a father because both of them undertook my same path, that is to say, they attended and successfully finished college (both in Cuba and in the former Soviet Union). They followed my example in concluding their studies in the same foreign countries. My daughter in the city of Lvov – Ukraine – and my son in Moscow – Russia – both formerly part of the Soviet Union. They finished their degrees at almost the same time I finished my two doctoral degrees in Kiev – Ukraine. They have always been useful citizens to themselves and to the societies where they resided. They are very highly prepared in their professions. Despite living in different countries – Rosita in Cuba, and Tonito in the United States – they always take care of their mother both economically and humanly as their children. Rosita directly takes care of her mother and continues living in Cuba. She did not have any children. I have not seen her since I emigrated from my country of origin on January 31, 1996. Nonetheless, we keep in contact through telephone calls and emails. My son lives in the United States. He is a good father, husband, and a successful businessman with impeccable credit and financial ratings. He is considerably dedicated to educating his intelligent daughter and watching her health and studies. She is an excellent student and outstanding athlete specializing in swimming. Furthermore, he, his wife – Olia – and the whole family are in very good standing in the state of Florida. They both achieved the American dream. I love my two children, and they love me, and – although sometimes there have been some partial misunderstandings in our paternal and fraternal relations – I feel blessed to be their father. I am proud of both of them. Between my son and me, there is an unusual but favorable relation. I was his mentor during his primary and secondary education in Havana, and now Tonito is my financial advisor in computing and electronic issues in which he is a highly qualified specialist. The relation with my daughter is more complex because she resides in Cuba, and my return to my motherland (even as a visitor) is permanently excluded due to deep political discrepancies – which are narrated in my book *Havana-Merida-Chicago* (A Journey to Freedom). During 2016-2017, I tried to invite my daughter to come to Chicago for a month, but the American

Embassy, located in Havana at the time, denied her the visa to come visit her father whom she has not seen for 24 years. In conclusion, my two children are my inspiration as a father.

Gladys Morales, my wife since 1976, showed me what real love is. With her support and care, I have become a better man. One of the manifestations of her love was to help me overcome my shortcomings as a man, as well as her insistence in helping me to rectify my many mistakes. She did not hesitate in fostering analyses or even peaceful arguments whose final objectives were to make me understand the importance of doing away with involuntary misbehaviors and lack of empathy toward other people. With patience and deep love, SHE DID TRANSFORM ME. Back in 1976, when we were dating, she gave me a copy of Victor Hugo's *Les Miserables* which impacted my life and relationships with my students, my co-workers, my peers, and my children. Since the moment we met and started our relationship, I have seen her love grow and grow and grow. I discover a new and fascinating feature of her personality every day, even after she passed away on October 5, 2015. I feel that I am falling in love with her again and again. This is because she IS an exceptional wife. She is my inspiration as a source of love. I recommend my readers the book I wrote to her – *Gladys, My Unforgettable Love* – in order to get deeper into Gladys's exceptionalism as a wife.

Teresa Nuñez Malvárez, my wife's special aunt, became the head of the family after her parents' deaths. She managed the family business. She contributed considerably to my wife's education and strong moral principles. For 23 years, she was confined to a wheelchair due to a serious neurological disease. Even though she could not walk, she continued to make the financial decisions for the family. She was able to keep the family together with a deep sense of respect and love. Her illness was painful. She was suffering tremendously – to the point of often having to spend days in the hospital. Nonetheless, she always encouraged others; she was able to turn a conversation about her sufferings into a conversation about the other person's life interests. Her education did not go beyond secondary school, but her adherence to principles and morals amounted to a degree from the University of Life. She died in the early 1980s, but she remains my inspiration in the courage and resistance to suffering that she demonstrated as well as an inspiration for instilling a sense of respect and mutual consideration in the family members.

Reverend Edgar Morales, my spiritual father since 1996, showed me what a true priest is. He is a man whose sermons invigorate my soul and whose kindness emanates from every word he pronounces and every gesture he makes. He is somebody who showed a great deal of patience and resignation at the moment when sickness overwhelmed his body but who never became depressed or lost his strong faith in God. When I arrived in Chicago after getting back to God in Mexico, I was confused by the large number of religions and the variety of Christian denominations here. Reverend Morales was the instrument the Lord used to get me into the church. He taught me to adore the Lord, to praise the Lord, and to be a better parishioner. He is my inspiration as a priest whose religious impact on my life will last forever even though he is not living in Chicago.

Gabriel de Jesus has been my friend and spiritual son since 1996. We became friends shortly after my arrival in Chicago. He was a student in my Spanish class, and he extended his helping hand at the moment when my wife and I needed it most. Our friendship began in Chicago between July and October of 1996 when he moved to Florida. Despite the distance, whenever he called us, it was as if we had not stopped seeing each other during the intervening years. When I had a heart attack in September, 1998, he was the first person to call me and offer his generous financial help. We shared our first Christmas in the U.S.A. with him and his lovely wife when they invited us to stay with them in Boca Raton. He is my inspiration as a friend and spiritual son.

Paul Maggio has been a friend of ours since 1996. He took classes in Spanish from my wife. He came into our lives while we were adapting to the American lifestyle, and his helping hand stretched far into the following year's right up to the present moment. Paul is the kind of friend one could trust without any sort of hesitation. He is an honest, open-minded man with a stable, friendly, and optimistic attitude, willing to listen and give sound advice. I witnessed his great inspiration as a friend when Gladys and I visited him in Puerto Rico to participate in his wedding. There, we met his lifelong friends who had traveled to Puerto Rico just to be with him on that special occasion. Some of them had been his friends since childhood, and they are still steadfast friends. I have never known a better example of an inspirational friend who routinely walks the talk when he offers, "Of course, I can help you." Paul is our inspiration as a friend.

The Mehmedi Family has also been an inspiration to me. I met Mr. Adrian Mehmedi when he was an undergraduate student in a course about Introductory Macroeconomics. After the quarter was over, I presented a talk about *Havana-Merida-Chicago* which Adrian attended. He purchased the book, read it, and gave it to his family. His father, Fadil Mehmedi, met me some days later. He and his wife, Shpresa, had read the book and wanted to meet me and my wife, and our friendship was born. Last summer, Fadil and Shpresa invited us for a memorable weekend holiday in Wisconsin and Iowa, and last week, in 2010, they celebrated their 25th wedding anniversary. Gladys and I were part of an unforgettable family party that included more than 75 people. All the invited guests except us were members of the family. I had never experienced such a genuine and solid family celebration. All the family participated in preparing the food. It was obvious that the entire 75-member family was enjoying and celebrating the wedding anniversary. Everybody not only enjoyed the party but actively participated in it. I was moved by the sincere and spontaneous gathering in the Mehmedi family which stood out as an inspirational family, able to intertwine love and respect in an exemplary way.

Samuel Betances, Hispanic community leader, became my friend in 1998. I met Samuel when he offered a workshop at St. Augustine College. His inspirational enthusiasm was transmitted to me and he showed me how to inspire an audience to take positive action in their lives. I translated his book *Ten Steps to the Head of the Class* from English into Spanish shortly after I had the heart attack. This was a crucial moment in developing my self-esteem because it was my rebirth into a new life. His effective work to foster diversity has touched many lives. He is my inspiration as a motivational speaker, in particular – although not limited – to the Hispanic population in the U.S. From an analysis of the common features of each of my inspirational models, I can draw some generalizations about the characteristics of inspirational people, which include the following traits:

a. Inspirational people should be role models in some field of activity.

b. Inspirational people must show tenacity and perseverance in setting an example.

c. Inspiration in the field of activity must become a part of the person's personality.

d. Inspirational people become inspirations through deeds, not words. Words and body language embellish an inspirational person's actions, but it is indispensable that the words and body language closely correspond to the deeds.

e. The time required to become an inspirational person may take days or weeks, but the impact must last forever. When I say forever, I mean it must endure beyond the death of the person.

f.  An inspirational person must have a main mission to fulfill in life, even though there is always more to do.

g.  Inspirational people must have the motivation and tenacity to face obstacles and learn how to overcome setbacks. They must welcome inconveniences, because such setbacks will help them grow and prepare them for bigger endeavors in the future.

h.  Inspirational people know that sometimes competitors may help them do a better job because competitors 'raise the bar' and force inspirational people to enhance their own capabilities.

i.  Inspirational people must be flexible and ready to change as long as their principles are not compromised.

j.  Inspirational people are willing both to talk and to listen. They welcome feedback because it allows them to know how effectively their message has gotten across to the target audience.

For people to be inspirational, they need at least one person to feel their impact. Not everybody is ready to be inspired. The best teacher cannot inspire each and every student. The ability to inspire is not the same in everybody. The level of inspiration depends on the receptivity of the person to be inspired. There is a mutual relationship between the inspirer and the inspired. These considerations bring us to the characteristics of those who are to be inspired. Let us assume that an inspirational individual is placed before a heterogeneous group of people who might be responsive to inspiration. My experience as a teacher and research leader for 54 years enables me to identify the features of those who respond well to inspiration. These include the following types of people:

a) People involved in an activity must show their willingness and ability to undertake it. They have to enjoy the activity and make it their own.

b) They should consciously or unconsciously take up the motivational traits they are being exposed to.

c) They should be motivated, allured to, or at least have to somewhat admire the one who is trying to inspire them.

d) Their spirit cannot give up on the activity.

e) They must be receptive to the impact of the inspirer. Patience, courage, and tenacity play a big role in determining how deep the effect on the inspired will be.

The aforementioned characteristics of inspirational people and people responsive to inspiration lead us to the following conclusions:

1. Inspirational people must be 'self-starters.' If they cannot inspire themselves, they will never be able to instill inspiration in others. Inspirational people must have experience facing obstacles and skill overcoming them, otherwise they will not be able to get their messages across.

2. When life deals an ugly hand to inspirational people, they must find inner motivation and courage to face the situation; they must think outside the box, utilize their full potential, weather the storm, and reach the safe shore.

3. Inspirational people must enjoy the process of instilling courage and tenacity in an audience. Their drive must be transparent and immediately felt.

4. Human beings can be impacted by inspirational persons in different ways, and some people are very hard to inspire in certain directions.

5. An inspirational person is usually focused on one area, and, in some cases, the inspiration extends to more than one set of endeavors.

6. Some people are inspired in a particular area of interest, but this area is not necessarily the one that the inspirational person is dealing with.

7. It is hard to find somebody who cannot be inspired in at least one endeavor by an inspirational individual.

8. To need inspiration is a necessary, but not sufficient, condition to be inspired. People must find inspiration either within or outside of themselves.

9. People may have a latent need to be inspired, which becomes apparent if an inspirational person enters into their lives.

10. Truly inspirational people will remain inspirational until the end of their days, and the impact of their inspiration will prevail beyond death.

**Food for Thought**

Imagine yourself in a public place surrounded by some people. Please, meditate about these questions:

1. Would you feel motivated to inspire them in any direction?

2. Have you ever been inspired by somebody offering a talk?

In this chapter, you have learned what inspiration is all about. Now, do you have any idea of how it can be instilled in others? Is there a general approach to the process through which inspiration appears in our lives? You can find out in the next chapter. Go on, please.

# Chapter II
# The Process of Being Inspired

*"Motivation is the art of getting people to do what you want them to do because they want to do it."*

– Dwight D. Eisenhower
34th President of the United States

Inspiration is not an easy word to define. According to the Wikipedia, there are several different types of inspiration, such as artistic, biblical, creative, musical, and so on. To cite just one of them, which I find particularly interesting and comprehensive, go on reading:

**"Artistic Inspiration** refers to an unconscious burst of creativity in a literary, musical, or other artistic endeavor. Literally, the word means 'breathed upon,' and it has its origins in both Hellenism and Hebraism. The Greeks believed that inspiration came from the muses as well as the gods Apollo and Dionysus. Similarly, in the Ancient Norse religions, inspiration derives from the gods, such as Odin. Inspiration is also a divine matter in Hebrew poetics. In the *Book of Amos*, the prophet speaks of being overwhelmed

42

by God's voice and compelled to speak. In Christianity inspiration is a gift of the Holy Spirit."

The purpose of this book is not so much to attempt to define inspiration, but actually to explore how it motivates people to go forward in whatever matter they are undertaking, and for how long this process takes place. In this chapter, I intend to explain – from my experiences as a professor, an author, an inspirational speaker, and an inspired student – how I believe a person can be inspired, what the effect of inspiration is on the inspired person, and how long this inspirational impact may last.

## My Experience as a Professor over 55 Years

Fidel Castro's leadership style was characterized by taking shortcuts and bypassing the normal stages it takes to attain given goals. This *modus operandi* was transmitted to his ministers and their subordinates. They could not operate otherwise. If they thoroughly analyzed the different tasks to be tackled, chances were that they would be replaced.

In 1967, one semester before finishing my bachelor's degree, I was selected to be an instructor of Linear Algebra. The rationale for this decision, as it was explained to me, was that – my voluntary tutoring of schoolmates in different courses and my research projects as a provisional research fellow (such a fellow worked without a mentor) in the economic teams that Fidel Castro himself had created back in 1965 – showed that I had a knack for applied mathematics. I did not receive pedagogical training of any kind. I had only taken one course in Linear Algebra, which was taught by means of a deeply theoretical approach. I had to teach it, however, in a way that was more accessible to students of economics without formal mathematical backgrounds. My teaching debut was with three sections totaling 145 students. I clearly remember that I was so unprepared for the task that at the end of my first-class session, when a student asked me a question and addressed me as 'professor,' I did not realize that he was talking to me, and I turned around to see where the professor was.

How did I fare in meeting this huge challenge? Well, I would honestly say that I barely managed to survive. How was I able to do this? First of all, I had no choice. There was no substitute. At the time, I was absolutely indoctrinated in the system of Cuban communism, and I believed that teaching was a duty assigned to me by my country which I could not let down. I felt a social compulsion pressing on my conscience. Secondly, I loved sharing information with other people and getting my message across. In other words, I loved teaching and had a natural vocation for it.

Since I had always been a student committed to learning and consequently to succeeding in all my courses, I was surprised to learn that not all of my students were studying, that some of them were not able to answer simple mathematical questions, and that some of them would never be able to pass the course. Therefore, the reactions of the students to my teaching were varied. Some of them were strongly inspired by my teaching, but others simply did not care. In other words, the same teaching method had different effects on the students depending on their own backgrounds, interests, and intellectual development.

My first teaching experience forced me to study complex subjects on my own, without any previous

preparation, and equipped me for more difficult challenges in the future.

After teaching Linear Algebra for one semester, I taught Linear Programming and other operational-research courses without any outside guidance. Thanks to the fact that I knew English and all books were written in that language, I was able to put the course together. My inspiration had paid off.

From 1967 to 1993, besides the operational-research courses, I also taught courses in the methodology of economic-mathematical models and research methodology. During these 26 years, I could feel that the enthusiasm of my students had dwindled. The precarious economic situation of the Cuban economy and the collapse of the Soviet Union discouraged, not only students, but also instructors. The 'wonderful promised future' that the Cuban Communist Party had been talking about for so many years was not to be seen anywhere. The collapse of the Soviet bloc showed many Cubans that the accomplishments of the Cuban Revolution were made possible thanks to Soviet subsidies to the Cuban sugar industry and the importation of oil from the Soviet Union at below-market prices, not to the efficiency of the socialist system. So, it became one of the most fervent hopes of Cuban academics to be sent abroad. It was almost a dream to imagine living in a normal country without rationing of the most basic goods, perpetual scarcities, waiting in lines, and the systematic political rhetoric.

In my case, the ruin of the sugar industry seriously affected the work of the research team I had been leading from 1982 to 1991. The deceit I experienced in Fidel

Castro's leadership – as well as the opening of my eyes to the reality of the Cuban dictatorship – rendered my stay in Cuba unbearable. I had to look to new horizons beyond my country of origin. I had studied very hard and learned intensively, and I needed to deliver my knowledge. A Mexican university gave me this opportunity, and between 1993 and 1996, I spent three unforgettable years teaching students and doing research in Mexico. The motivation to actualize myself as a professor was immense. For me, actualization meant delivering knowledge that could be applied to the economic reality of a given country, in this case Mexico. The motivation to my students was also noticeable. I felt that all my capacities were unleashed after being repressed for so long in Cuba. However, I was not a free man in Mexico; I was subject to the decisions of the College of Economics of the University of Havana. Still, I was very inspired to be working as a professor in Mexico where I received the Cátedra Patrimonial de Excelencia – a grant awarded for excellence in research and teaching – from the Mexican government. The professor-student interaction was fantastic in Mexico.

In 1996, I finally severed my ties to the Cuban regime and arrived in Chicago. I worked ten years as an instructor of introductory economics at St. Augustine College, a junior college specializing in the education of the Hispanic immigrant community, and 12 years as an instructor of economics and international political economy at DePaul University. At St. Augustine College, I was inspired to teach students at a low college level but with high aspirations to succeed in America and to achieve the American dream. At DePaul University, I was inspired to teach undergraduate and graduate students who dreamed 'big' about finishing their bachelor and master's degrees. Although at St. Augustine College I found a degree of diversity among students of Hispanic origin, at DePaul University, I was meeting an even more diverse body of students from all continents. My inspiration to teach was totally fulfilled, and I believe that – in the majority of students – the inspiration to get ahead in America through the acquisition of knowledge is noticeable.

## Summarizing My Experience as a Professor

To be an inspirational professor, one needs to feel a profound love for acquiring and delivering knowledge in a comprehensible way. The issue is not to let people know how much one has learned. The point is to make people feel the passion for learning, to help them think in a more professional way, to develop reasoning skills, and – consequently – to enable them to learn. An inspiring professor lives each class session as a new experience. Each student is unique. Regardless of how many times a professor has explained a given topic, new ways to deliver the knowledge can be found every day, depending on the interest and the preparation of the majority of the students. The systematic preparation required to deliver high-level courses allows instructors to delve deeper and deeper into the subject matter and transmit that knowledge to students. I must say that sometimes after delivering a lecture that one could think of as creative, I have felt the need to sit down and enjoy the pleasure of having gotten my message across. After such a profound and rewarding experience, it is difficult just to go on and tackle the next task.

An inspirational professor can contribute considerably to fostering inspiration in students. The process starts in the very first class. The professor should be able to capture the students' attention, to make them forget time, and to make their classroom experience enjoyable. The inspirational professor should impress upon the students the importance of the habit of preparing themselves in the subject before attending class – at least through reading the chapters assigned in the textbook or in handouts distributed by the instructor. The professor should impress the students the need to participate during class time – in interactive classes – and the responsibility to study the material shortly after attending class – through homework, preparation for seminars, exams, and research paper.

Besides having an acceptable level of intelligence, a solid background in the subject matter, and good study habits, a student needs to be inspired to attain an 'A.' The inspiration helps the student to study when he or she does not feel like studying but might prefer to enjoy himself or herself at a party. The joy of learning and its realization in a good grade compensates for the sacrifice. An inspired student knows that to study is his or her most important responsibility and is the reason for being in college in the first place.

The effect of an inspirational professor on students is variable. It may last for moments or years depending on the students' resilience and internal motivation. It may be born in the classroom or developed in the classroom. It may continue over students' careers at the university and extend into their professional lives. Inspiration can even be immersed in their inner selves in such a way as to become a part of their personalities.

As personal examples, I will quote emails and letters sent to me by some of my students. The comments took place in the period 2006-2010.

a. A student in Introduction to Money and Banking in the fall quarter of 2006 wrote to me after he finished the course. He started to work in his professional field shortly after graduating as a finance major from DePaul University.

On November 23, 2006, Mr. Jeff Del Corse sent me the following email:

First of all, I would like to thank you for your congratulations. It was a tough course and I worked very, very hard. However, I couldn't have done it without your inspiration. So second of all, I would like to thank you for your great passion for teaching. Never before had I had a professor go to such great lengths in making sure that his or her students actually understand the material. I am usually very shy in class and don't like to participate, but, thanks to the way in which you helped students feel comfortable in explaining the material, I had no problem speaking in your class.

I have heard before that every student that goes through college will encounter one professor that they will always remember. You are that professor for me. I have learned more in your economics class than I have in any other class I have taken so far at DePaul.

One thing that you said during class will stick with me for the remainder of my career here at DePaul and someday when I have children in school: "It is not about the grade that you receive in the class, it's about how much you LEARN." I think that a lot of students (including myself prior to your class) go through college so worried about what their GPA was that they forget the reason why they're in college in the first place; to learn! So we cram for our exams the night before, and then after the exam we forget what it is that we studied for. From now on, I will have a new approach.

b. A student in Global Connections wrote to me after he finished the course in the fall quarter of 2008. This gentleman took two other courses with me in the following quarters and built the website for my book *Havana-Merida-Chicago* in 2010.

Mr. Scott Bruzek wrote on November 19, 2008.

Dear Dr. Morales-Pita:

I would like to thank you for the incredible influence that you have had on me over the past ten weeks. Because of this class – but more importantly – your unique approach to presenting the material, I felt extremely motivated and excited to continue my study of the global economy and its many related factors. In my education career, I have had no educator that has been more inspirational than you. You put your heart and soul into everything you do, all for the advancement of your students. I have a great deal of respect for everything you have experienced and done throughout your life. I feel as though it will be extremely difficult, if not impossible, to find a professor at DePaul University or any other university in the country, who brings such a unique perspective, but more importantly, more passion than I could even imagine, to his or her teaching.

I am absolutely delighted to take a microeconomics course from you in the winter quarter. While the content may not be involving as global economics, I have complete faith that I will enjoy the course just as much I did Global Connections.

I am not the only one that shares this view of your incredible teaching ability. I have talked to a number of students in the course who talk about how much more they understand the global economy, especially due to your stellar teaching. They regard you to the highest degree because of the inspiration you have toward your students.

I would also like to say that this class has not only taught me about the global economy and political relations, but I have learned even more about myself as a person. I have augmented my analytical skills, learned that every story has two sides to it, and worked to see the world in a new light. This has opened my eyes to the various issues I had remained blinded to before.

To end this letter, I would like to thank you for everything you have done to help me out, and I take pride in the fact that I can be a part of one of your most memorable classes ever. Neither time nor space allows me to say everything that I wish to say in this letter. In my next few years at DePaul, I wish that you would be a mentor of mine when I have questions regarding my future path in global economics and international studies. I would greatly appreciate this, as it is a testament to your incredible inspirational and educational ability.

c. A student who took Introduction to Microeconomics and Global Connections in the winter and spring quarters of 2009, and worked with me as a research fellow wrote me. He applied to continue his economic studies at the University of Chicago and was accepted.

Mr. David Hampton sent me the following email on May 17, 2010:

Dear Dr. Morales-Pita,

I hope that you and your wife have been doing well. I would like to sincerely thank you for writing my recommendation letter for the University of Chicago. I have recently been accepted and will begin as a student at U.C. this fall. I cannot tell you how excited I am to be a part of an economics program that has had such a substantial influence on modern economic thought and produced such brilliant minds in both economics and mathematics among many other fields!

I would like to thank you for igniting my passion for rigorous research. Indeed, I realized how passionate I was when working on my research for you, which led me to pursue a research institution like the University of Chicago. Not only have you inspired me academically but also on a personal level. Your story encouraged me to strive for what others thought was not possible and to focus on the pursuit of truth and knowledge. Attending the University of Chicago is the product of both of those ideas that you instilled in me.

Thank you.

d.   A student in the Focal Point – Karl Marx course in the winter quarter of 2010 – wrote to me. She was then a sophomore at DePaul University.

Ms. Becca Son sent me the following email on June 8, 2010:

Dear Professor Morales,

I'm sorry that we did not get a chance to talk to each other before the class ended, but I just wanted to email you about how much I enjoyed this class. The exportability of the knowledge I have gained has helped me tremendously in other courses this spring quarter. I am grateful for the knowledge you have placed and fostered in your students. Besides the learning experience, I would just like to say how refreshing and encouraging it was to have an instructor so passionate about his work and shaping minds. In my first year at DePaul, you have been one of the few professors out of many this year that made me see beyond the academic letter grade but enjoy the experience of what I am learning as well. I know this section was challenging for you, but, nonetheless, you were outspoken and passionate. I hope that I will have more opportunities to take a course instructed by you later in my academic career (I am an INT student). The essence of this email is to thank you for the experience. I hope our schedules cross paths again.

e. A student of the Seminar for Seniors in the 2009 fall quarter. In previous quarters, she had taken the courses Introduction to Macroeconomics and Introduction to Microeconomics with me. She held a professional position shortly after graduating as an International Studies major at DePaul University.

Ms. Kathleen di Martino sent this email on August 27, 2010:

I first entered Dr. Morales-Pita's Intro to Macroeconomics class with the same nervous energy that accompanied me at the beginning of every quarter. It was the anticipation of the unknown that made me anxious: the difficulty of the course, the personality of the professor, the amount of homework. I quickly learned that I would need to pay attention in Dr. Morales-Pita's class. Not only were the concepts challenging but the expectations were also high.

From the very first day, Dr. Morales-Pita encouraged us to study methodically, reading the assigned chapters before each class and reviewing our notes afterward. Throughout the course, he advised us against our preoccupations with grades; instead, we should focus on developing a deep understanding of the material. He taught us to do this by following a logical approach to each problem. We would not simply be memorizing formulas in this course, we would be learning how to think critically. And this is a skill that I have since found to be immensely valuable.

Through his class, I learned that only by applying myself to the material – as well as holding myself responsible for my education – would I succeed in school and in life. This meant prohibiting myself from excuses and managing my time better. It also meant recognizing when I needed help and then making the effort to seek it out. Dr. Morales-Pita was always available to his students, whether that meant staying late or scheduling additional study sessions for the class.

At first, the course seemed quite daunting. However, Dr. Morales-Pita's passion – for both his students and for economics – inspired me to explore the subject further. I went on to take several more economics courses as well as two more courses with Dr. Morales-Pita. The final class I took with him was my senior seminar, the culmination of my studies at DePaul. There were only six students in that class, and our task was to produce a comprehensive study of the economic, social, and political factors that pushed Latin American countries toward populism. This seemed nearly impossible at the time. Eventually, I realized that Dr. Morales-Pita had assigned such a complex research project because he knew something that we did not. He knew that we were capable of success. By the end of the quarter, I had a 38-page report that Dr. Morales-Pita helped me to publish in an online – www.cubanalisis.com Think Tank along with two of his other students.

I am so thankful to have had Dr. Morales-Pita as a professor. Although I have always been a good student, you could say that he helped me to learn how to learn and inspired me to approach my goals with determination. Rather than cramming for tests and fulfilling the minimum for that 'A,' he motivated me to approach each new assignment as an opportunity. As a result of his teachings, I refuse to settle. Instead, I will push myself further and overcome whatever obstacles may stand in my way. His life experience is an example of tenacity that I aspire to follow.

f.    The most impressive email, though, was sent by a student who did research work under my supervision. He jointly participated with me in an international seminar in September, 2009, giving a presentation that was some months later published by an international journal in Poland. Although his major was Political Science, his experience with me directed his orientation toward Economics and

International Political Economy. Then, he was starting a master's degree in Econometrics in one of the most renowned universities in China.

Below is Mr. Sidney Evans's August 20, 2010, email from Beijing, China, sent to somebody I had referred him to:

As a student living in the most privileged country in the world, it is all too common to take one of the greatest gifts in life, education, for granted. Sometimes, one felt like floating through life with the end goal of happiness, wealth, and knowledge but no real guidance in the skills required to reach these goals. This was indeed the case for me – as well as many others in similar situations. The question is, 'what does it take to break this cycle?' For me, it was one man, Antonio Morales-Pita. I met him while taking a basic-level international studies class at DePaul University. Dr. Morales-Pita saw something in me; he has since told me after my work with him that he saw I possessed the ability to be inspired. I thank my blessings every day for possessing this trait or at least that he believed I possessed it.

Mentoring is not a narrowly focused word for Dr. Morales-Pita; he approaches mentoring in its totality. Dr. Morales-Pita not only mentors from an educational standpoint but mentors youth in the fields of life, love, attitude, hard work, and respect for all that life offers. I began my work with Dr. Morales-Pita as a boy looking for answers. While I continue to receive his mentoring, as a result of the time and work, I can say he has helped me become a man with all the skills necessary to be successful in any endeavor that life offers. For Dr. Morales-Pita, mentoring is not just a word; it is a way of life. The inspiration that Dr. Morales offers is not just through the story of his incredible life and the heartache he has endured but his ability to become inspired along with a student when he or she achieves a goal or makes a positive chance in their life.

Dr. Morales-Pita possesses the ability to instruct students in the fields mentioned above, but the most valuable skill he offers students is not given through words. It is instilled in them by his unwavering example of a man that every person in the world should attempt to emulate. I attribute much of who I am today to Dr. Morales-Pita. The life lessons he offers should be taken to heart by all people in all walks of life, because Dr. Morales-Pita is not only an incredible mentor but the most incredible human being I have ever had the pleasure of meeting in my life.

g. Another example comes from somebody who never sat down in any of my classes. The person – whose testament of inspiration as a student I am about to quote – had not even met me previously. She was inspired to pursue her GED studies while reading *Havana-Mérida-Chicago*. She is one of these persons who can be inspired to study because she loves to learn and to grow intellectually. This is her story. On January 27, 2010, I received an unexpected email from a person I had not met. The subject of the email was 'Thank you.' This was the content of that email from Ms. Erika Urquiza:

Hi, how are you? I hope that with God's help you and your wife, Gladys, are doing well. Let me introduce myself. My name is Erika.

From the bottom of my heart, I hope that you can read this email. Maybe you are too busy, but hope is the last thing that a human being can lose. The reason for this email is to thank your wife and you. Let me explain.

A couple of days ago I found your book. From the very first moment, I could not stop reading it. It was like a film. I felt the need to know more about your life. I needed to live every event in your life. I could not omit a single word. Your book inspired me to keep my hope alive.

I am the mother of three children whom I raise with my husband. Due to various circumstances, I had never had the opportunity to study. I am a Mexican immigrant who came to this country to live a better life, but for an unknown reason, somewhere in this journey I stopped dreaming.

Unfortunately, my family did not have the resources required for studying, but thanks God I always had the internal need to learn. Originally, I enrolled myself in English as a second-language course. I am doing reasonably well, but reading your book persuaded me to do more. I have just enrolled in a GED course and maybe in the near future I can go to college.

I started my email thanking your wife and you because I imagine that she is one of the main reasons for writing this marvelous book. This piece of literature has provided me with energy and strength to go on with my life as a student. Just shortly before reading your book, I was thinking about stopping trying to pursue my dreams and my goals. I have just finished reading your book and tried to get your email.

I couldn't wait even a day to let you know that your book makes the reader live, laugh, cry. I really got emotional when – after a seven-month sag – you could finally return to Mexico and meet your beloved Gladys after you had been separated by the Cuban regime. I was also impacted by the way you were hiding from the Mexican immigration. I was devastated when, despite your contribution to the Mexican educational system, you were not receiving the respect and support that you so genuinely deserved.

Because of this influence, and even not being sure whether you will read this email, I thank you for being an angel who whispered in my ear, "Don't give up, don't lose your faith, and get ahead."

With deep respect and admiration,

Sincerely,
Erika Urquiza

Erika's being inspired by my book shows that a person can be inspired not only through direct experience but also through the work of an inspirational human being.

It goes without saying that I was strongly impacted by this email. According to this testimony, I had been able to transform myself into a book and to inspire an unknown person to get on with her life and to continue studying.

Some 35 years ago, my then-fiancée Gladys gave me the book *Les Miserables* by Victor Hugo. Reading this book inspired me to modify my then-strongly exacting and highly demanding attitude as a teacher into a more flexible, understanding yet nonetheless demanding one. Victor Hugo masterfully described Policeman Javert's tenacious intolerance to chase a man who stole a piece of bread from an open window. I saw myself reflected in this mirror and came to the conclusion that I was unfairly harsh and needed to modify this negative side of my personality. I recognized that I needed to change my intolerant attitude as a teacher for the better while keeping my ethical personality as an educator. Victor Hugo wrote *Les Miserables* before 1885, and he was inspiring a young instructor 125 years later. The underlying story of *Havana-Mérida-Chicago* was based on his book. I tried to write a book that would show how a man's life is changed by historical events lived in different countries under different political and economic conditions. Only Heaven knows how many people have changed their lives for the better under the influence of this famous French writer!

## My Experience as a Student

I consider myself to be an inspired student. My mother developed in me the love for reading and studying. Whenever I was sitting in a classroom, all my attention was concentrated on the instructor. Whether I was studying English, mathematics, biology, or shorthand, I really enjoyed being in class. When I had inspirational teachers in high-school mathematics and in ancient history, they increased my desire to learn and instilled in me the need to study and to get good grades. If I had teachers whose pedagogic abilities were not very strong, I made the extra effort and found additional knowledge in textbooks that complemented the incomplete, incoherent, or deficient lectures of the classroom. My goal was always to achieve scores above 89 points, regardless of the circumstances that surrounded my learning experience.

During my undergraduate studies in economics at the University of Havana, I was taught by just a few inspirational professors – in calculus and operational research (three out of the nearly 40 instructors I had) – but my grades included 37 'A's' and three 'B's.' I felt the need to get these scores. I always thought that 70% was a very low requirement for passing a course.

Three years after finishing my baccalaureate degree, I was chosen to do graduate work in the United Kingdom. The Lord made it possible that the United Nations offered a scholarship to a student at the University of Havana to study operational research in Great Britain. Although there were five instructors in the Operational Research Department of the College of Economics in 1969, I was the only one who knew English; consequently, I was sent to Glasgow, Scotland. In the graduate program in Glasgow, I was the only student that was not a native speaker of English.

While in Scotland, I realized that the lectures and exams that I was giving to my students in Cuba were totally different from those delivered at Strathclyde University. Firstly, the lecturers hardly interacted with students in the classroom. Very few questions were asked by the students. The blackboard was a mobile structure which the instructors filled and rolled without even turning their attention to the students. I noticed that the majority of the instructors did not show any interest in student learning. The learning process was the total responsibility of students. If the students had questions, their only option was to ask for an appointment with the instructor. There were no office hours.

To sum up the experience, there was no inspiration from the instructor to the students. They had to inspire themselves.

Secondly, the exams were taken under huge pressure. The exams themselves offered a choice to the students. Each exam was divided into three sections and contained nine or ten questions, and each student had to choose a minimum and maximum number of questions in each section under a British-time regime. So each student had to precisely calculate the time to finish each question in order to answer five of them in a couple of hours. After finishing each exam, I felt as if I had a horse riding inside my brain. I was virtually panting and had to rest a while after completing an exam. In conclusion, the exams showed how efficiently a human being could take an exam when he or she is under intense pressure. There was no time for getting nervous or for asking any question to the proctor.

Despite these non-inspiring circumstances, I was inspired to get good grades because I received this task 'from my country,' as I seriously believed at the time. I had to teach my peers at the Department of Operational Research all the courses I was learning, so I studied very hard from the very first day of classes and had outstanding academic results in my degree. My inspiration had paid off.

After turning 33 years old, I was inspired to study Russian intensely for two reasons: my only opportunity to hold a Ph.D. degree was to write my dissertation and defend it in the former Soviet Union, and I needed to translate books and articles from Russian into Spanish in order to accrue the necessary funds to get married to the woman in my life.

Analyzing the two experiences as an inspired instructor and student, it can be concluded that to be inspired in an academic context requires the following:

a) the need to take action – to teach or to study;
b) the ability to undertake that action – to have the necessary knowledge and training;
c) sufficient motivation to take action – through internal and/or external stimulus;
d) the tenacity to take action and stick to it until the final result is achieved;
e) the readiness to overcome obstacles and to see them as opportunities rather than challenges.

I would also like to add that not everybody can be inspirational, and not everybody can be inspired. Anybody, however, may feel the need to be inspirational about something he or she is good at, and almost anybody can be inclined to be inspired if he or she finds the right inspirational person and is mentally disposed to receive the message. Most people experience the need and motivation to take action.

Inspiration can germinate as long as there is a scenario in which:

a) somebody has the motivation to take action, is convinced that it is suitable to do so, and is ready to undertake a systematic program to reach the goal;
b) somebody is able to motivate the person to take a course of action or is able to elicit receptivity in the

person toward pursuing some goal and is able to get his or her point across to the recipient.

It is important to recognize that motivation doesn't necessarily have to originate with somebody who is personally connected to the individual in the process of being inspired. It can be triggered by a good book, an article in a newspaper, an inspiring diary, a film, or a moving, artistic performance.

When I saw Susan Boyle performing on *Britain's Got Talent*, she inspired me. My inspiration was not related to any pride I take in singing (by the way, I started singing in public in 2015 after my wife's death since up to that time I was not aware to have any talent in that area). My inspiration went beyond admiration of an outstanding performance. My inspiration was related to the fact that she represented a human being, coming from a small town (or 'a collection of villages' – as Susan put it when she appeared on the T.V. broadcast) yet possessing an outstanding talent and the courage and tenacity to perform in front of millions of people and a demanding group of judges.

She was able to succeed, to make the judges and entire audience rise to give her a prolonged round of applause. It did not matter that her age and her shape were not typical of a rising star. It did not matter that people were laughing when she said that she wanted to become a professional singer and that her ideal was to sing like Elaine Page. She dreamed big.! Today, Susan Boyle is a worldwide star with more than 48 million viewers on YouTube as of August 27, 2010.

Getting a book published by a conventional publisher is hard for an author who is not a celebrity. Susan Boyle gave me the inspiration to continue to looking for a publisher for *Havana-Merida-Chicago*, and she also gave me the motivation to write this book.

The inspiration may last a second, a week, a year, or a lifetime. The strength of such a reciprocal need felt by a pair of individuals and the solidness of their motivation determines the duration and resilience of this wonderful human experience.

By now, you should be aware of the importance of tenacity and the magical effect of inspiration. This chapter has been quite general in its discussion of inspiration. Let us now set our minds on three concrete examples of inspiration that will help you better understand this wondrous and useful quality. Chapters III, IV, and V await you. They will quench your thirst to know more about the process of inspiration and show you how to be inspirational in your specific areas of interest. Prepare yourself to become emotional as you feel your capacity to inspire and to be inspired grows while you read and analyze – and meditate on – the contents to come. You are just two pages away from the first classroom example.

# Second Part
# Examples of Inspiration in the Classroom and at Home

# Chapter III

# How to Inspire Students to Accomplish Their Educational Goals?

*"The only person who is educated is the one who has learned how to learn…and change."*

– Carl Rogers
Influential Psychologist

"The things taught in schools and colleges are not an education, but the means to an education."

– Ralph Waldo Emerson
Transcendental Essayist

To study is the best way to break the cycle of poverty, to expand one's understanding of the world, and to become a better and more proficient human being. The process of learning requires two sets of agents who complement each other: instructors on one hand, and students on the other hand.

# An Inspiring Educator

To be an inspiring educator is not an easy task. I had many instructors in primary, middle school, high school, universities, research institutes, and language institutes. It is not easy to determine how many of them imparted their knowledge to me, but the number of fingers on my right hand is more than enough to count those who have impacted my life: these were the truly inspiring educators. Although students should systematically study regardless of the quality of their instructors, it certainly helps to be taught by a good educator.

Based on my personal experience in classrooms both as a student and an instructor, I can enumerate the characteristics that define an inspiring educator who must be able to:

a) attract and maintain the attention and respect of students at all times;

b) deliver an understandable lecture in an organized manner and using both an inductive (going from the particular to the general) approach and a deductive (going from the general to the particular) approach;

c) be knowledgeable in the subject matter and its practical application;

d) include theoretical examples as part of the class;

e) try to reach every student regardless of different educational backgrounds – this especially applies to freshmen;

f) read the students' eyes to find out whether they are following the explanations;

g) ask questions that will directly or indirectly show that the average student is following the main points of the lecture;

h) welcome questions as a way to interact with the students, realizing that no question is silly if it is honestly asked;

i) care about the students and make sure that they really understand the subject matter;

j) encourage perfect attendance by delivering interesting and useful lectures in class as well as factoring attendance into the grade for the course;

k) develop the analytical and cognitive skills of the students;

l) teach students to think outside the box by using innovative approaches to problems;

m) prepare students to master theory to solve problems they will later encounter in their professional lives;

n) recognize one's own faults or mistakes, because students generally expect their instructors to be human beings, not infallible teaching machines who know all the answers;

o) learning for its own sake over studying to get a grade. Make it clear to students that their main function in the class is to learn, not only to pass the course, and that if they study to learn, they will definitely pass the exams, but if they study only to pass the exams, they will soon forget what they have studied;

p) inspire students to attempt to achieve the highest possible grades as a way to learn;

q) be exacting, but add a human touch; demonstrate flexibility within pedagogical principles;

r) require students to continue to study beyond the walls of the classroom;

s) explain to students that the work of the instructor cannot substitute for the effort and hard work that students themselves must do to develop their intelligence and skill level, and that the real learning process takes place when students are able to solve the problems assigned by the instructor on their own;

t) emphasize in the syllabus and guidelines on grading that students should follow the three phases of learning: studying the material before class, attending class as well as actively participating in class discussions, and studying the material after class;

u) be fair, impartial, and transparent in the evaluation process, allowing students to know why they lost points and how to avoid the same mistake from occurring again.

As can be seen, it is very hard to be an inspirational educator who will be remembered and well thought of after the course is over. In a nutshell, an inspirational educator is one who holds the attention of his or her students, makes the class enjoyable and useful, instills in the students the need to do their best both in and out of the class, and emphasizes learning the subject over passing the course. It is the educator who paves the way for the making of future scientists. It is the instructor who – while engaged in research work, publishing papers, and participating in conferences and seminars – makes teaching his priority. He sees a part of himself in his or her students' papers, theses, and dissertations.

Now I will discuss the other part of the inspirational equation, i.e., the student who is open to inspiration.

## A Student Who is Able to Be Inspired

Is it easy to inspire students, helping them develop their learning skills, discipline, and respect for instructors and peers? The answer is, emphatically, no. A student is also a family member and is enrolled in several other courses during a quarter or a semester. A student may have personal and health problems, may be a procrastinator, or may turn in homework with spelling and grammatical mistakes.

The best students are usually found among those who get As and Bs in the exams and on their papers, but sometimes an inspiring educator can help transform a struggling student into an outstanding one.

The best student is that individual who goes to class to learn, gets a good grade (not necessarily an 'A'), and is able to apply his or her knowledge to real-life problems as a professional.

What are the characteristics of students who want to be inspired and can even inspire their instructors?

Such students must:

- punctually attend at least 90% of the class sessions, only taking absences when they have a legitimate reason;

- learn the subject matter in the three required phases (before, during, and after class);
- be able to allocate their study time among all their courses, making the tougher ones a priority but giving the easier ones sufficient attention as well;
- study and reason outside the box;
- read newspapers and articles in specialized journals, listen to T.V. news broadcasts and programs intended to raise the viewer's intellectual level, and bring interesting questions to the classroom;
- participate in class by asking and answering questions;
- deliver papers and assignments on time;
- score $\geq 80\%$ in every exam or category on which they are graded.

The above characteristics apply to students committed to learning and most likely to be impacted by inspirational instructors. It is not often that an instructor will teach a section with more than 40% of the students who possess the aforementioned characteristics, but when this favorable scenario coincides with an inspirational instructor, the results may be exceptionally good.

During the 2008 fall quarter at DePaul University, I had an INT-150 section of students who met these conditions. Every class was like an adventure in which students and the instructor became a cohesive body solely interested in learning, contributing to the individual and collective learning process, asking interesting questions beyond the limits of the textbook, and giving top-quality presentations and papers. I still maintain contact with some of these students with whom I have also worked on joint research projects.

Unfortunately, sometimes one finds students whose only purpose is to pass a course without making the requisite effort, missing classes and assignments and consequently getting poor scores on exams. These students are very hard to inspire because their interests do not coincide with those of the instructor.

The aforementioned considerations lead us to conclude that in order to be inspired, students must:

1) be interested in learning and not only in passing the course;
2) understand the need to be inspired which may arise from their vocational aspirations, career orientations, or financial interests;
3) have good study habits or be willing to improve them by following the advice of the instructor;
4) understand that education is an investment made by students, their families, and/or governments, and that students should strive to be at the top of the class to justify the resources invested in them;
5) accept academic challenges as opportunities for growth, not as hindrances.

**Food for Thought**

Invitation to meditate:

1. In your opinion, which are the main conclusions of this chapter?

2. Have you had any similar inspirational experience in a classroom?

History and literature show that parents exert a strong influence on the academic development of their children. Having gotten acquainted with the inspirational process that occurs between students and instructors, let us explore the foundations for education – the home and the parents. The next chapter is devoted to parents and their children.

# Chapter IV

# How to Inspire Parents to Become Role Models in Education for Their Children?

*"The important thing is not so much that every child should be taught, as that every child should be given the wish to learn."*

– John Lubbock,
English Banker, Politician, Biologist, and Archeologist

While in Seville last summer, I was listening to a Televisión Española broadcast describing Mario Vargas Llosa's way of writing, and heard the following line: "Every personal story is a family story." This was one of the most succinct and clear expressions I have ever heard that refers to the powerful influence that parents and family environments exert on human beings. Whenever one reads or hears the story of a celebrity in whatever context, the family influence pops up right away as a source inspiration.

Children mimic their parents' behaviors, especially if there is a direct correspondence between words and deeds. Parents who never smoke and advise their offspring about the harm of smoking to health would most likely foster non-smokers. Parents who are positively disposed toward education, who instill in their children the need to learn, the joy of acquiring knowledge, and the honor of being at the head of the class, who support their children's studies, encourage and demand good academic results according to their children's capabilities, and who support their actions with words of advice and acknowledgment of progress will become important role models in the education of their children. From observations over my 45-year career as a teacher, oftentimes good students are individuals whose parents (or at least one parent) were role models in their education.

What does it mean to become a role model in the education of a child and why is this critically important? If parents become role models in the education of their children, they will remain a source of inspiration that outlasts their own lives. Respect and admiration will strengthen the children's love for their parents and will deter the children from unacceptable social behavior. Children will be proud to follow in their parents' footsteps and will likely do their best not to embarrass or shame their parents by bad behavior.

To ascend on the educational ladder implies sacrifice, tenacity, and the courage to accept and to overcome challenges. Consequently, becoming role models in their children's education will also help parents raise good citizens.

The ideal situation would be for both the father and the mother to become role models in the education for their children. If they are able to maintain a stable marriage, their influence will be even greater. Nonetheless, love between a man and a woman may last forever or be of limited duration. Although oftentimes divorce engenders acrimonious relations between the father and the mother, the relationship between a parent and child does not have to be disrupted by a divorce between parents. Both members of the couple should be interested in raising a happy and educated child. My experience as a divorced and loving father who became a role model in the education for his children shows that it is possible for a single parent to remain an educational role model.

On the basis of my personal experience facilitating workshops for parents in the Chicago Public Schools (under the sponsorship of the Bilingual Parents Resource Center of the Chicago Public School system between 2007 and 2009), as a role model in the education of my children and as a child whose mother became a role model in her son's education, I can enumerate the characteristics that define what an inspiring parent needs to become an educational role model while their child is in primary or secondary school. This is an individual who is able to:

a) participate directly (by helping with the children's homework and explaining the subject matter) or indirectly (by seeking other people who have the necessary educational background to help) in the academic activities of his or her children;

b) visit the school, talk to the teachers, and be up to date on their children's academic standing in the classroom before and after exams;

c) actively participate in all parent-teacher meetings at school;

d) demand good academic results from their children according to their capabilities, recognize these good results, and encourage their children to persevere be tenacious in difficult courses even if the results are below expectations;

e) give up material things for the sake of supporting the costs of education – in other words, show their children that education is an investment in the future;

f) create favorable study conditions at home, such as a specific place for studying, free of T.V. distraction, with good lighting;

g) foster good study habits such as punctual attendance in classes, routine dedication to homework during weekdays, avoidance of procrastinating and cramming before exams, and getting enough sleep and rest during weekends;

h) schedule, with the children's participation and acceptance, times for study and for watching T.V. programs;

i) assign academic assignments (such as reading book and discussion of educational materials) over vacation breaks;

j) foster reading habits and the creation of a reading club at home with the participation of all family members and possibly some friends;

k) organize visits to museums and to educational talks and workshops;

l) undertake studies on one's own to improve his or her chances of getting a better job and thereby to set another positive example for the children;

m) study on his or her own and see these studies successfully through to completion;

n) celebrate the academic successes of the children according to the family's material circumstances.

In a nutshell, an inspirational parent, who is able to become a role model in the education of his or her children, is in reality an educator whose love for the children expresses itself not only by showing affection but also by understanding their problems, inspiring confidence in them, raising their self-esteem, supporting their educational endeavors, and teaching them how to welcome challenges and overcome obstacles. Such parents inspire their children to do their best in and out of class and to set learning as a priority over passing. This task is not at all easy, but the reward is huge.

As in any inspirational situation, it takes 'two to tango,' so, given that a parent is ready to become a role model in the education of his or her children, we must ask whether every child is ready and willing to welcome an inspiring parent? If a child's behavior is normal and the child does not face adverse circumstances at home or at school, most likely the child will respond positively to a parent committed to becoming a role model in the child's education.

Given the fact that – besides being subject to parental influence – every child has his or her own inclinations and preferences, it is especially important in this inspirational equation that parents understand their children's abilities and talents and give their support to the child's inclination in this direction. A parent having a successful career as a medical doctor doesn't necessarily have a child who will grow up to be a physician. A top-quality singer or composer should not expect to raise an artist. It is oftentimes found that professionals give rise to professional offspring, but the professions their offspring pursue are not necessarily the same.

Some parents try to force their children to follow in their career paths, at times eliciting frustration in their children. To become role models in children's education does not mean making children follow in the same footsteps as their parents, but it does mean that, by becoming educational role models, parents help develop good study habits in their children and nurture professional aspirations in their children according to their intellectual capacities and gifts.

Becoming role models in education is so important and decisive that even parents of limited education – who had no access to education in their childhood for reasons beyond their control – can foster the desire in their children to enter and finish college with flying colors.

My mother, Siria Pita Allende, as a child born to a poor family, could not attend grade school, let alone college, but she always had the desire to learn. She felt frustrated because she was unable to read books and newspapers, but she was an intelligent woman. My father, Florentino Morales, was a remarkably intelligent man who came from a similar situation. He grew up in a family of a single mother and three children living in a rural area outside of Havana. His father died when Florentino was a child. He started to work as a farmer and horse tamer at age eight. When Florentino married Siria, they informally but effectively agreed to share family responsibilities in the following way: Florentino would take care of supporting the family materially while Siria would be a housewife responsible for the education and care of the children.

Florentino (who only possessed an understanding of commercial mathematics and basic reading skills) and Siria (an illiterate mother) were able to raise four children, all of whom entered and finished college at the University of Havana.

Siria Pita did a good job and became the role model for the family. Her children were the first to attend college in either of the two branches of the Morales-Pita family. How was this possible? It is common that most parents wish for their children a better life than they themselves had. Siria Pita defined a better life for her children as being educated, working in an office or in a school, in other words becoming 'white collar' workers, or possibly running their own businesses. The communist revolution in Cuba put an end to private ownership, but not to intellectual careers.

To enumerate some of the ways Siria Pita promoted her children's education, I list the following. She:

1.  Actively participated in school, not only in school meetings but in private office hours with the teachers. She needed to know how her children were doing grade-wise and in their relationships with their teachers and peers.

2. Fostered systematic study habits at home and required her children to visit libraries during summer breaks.
3. Insisted they study music and take piano lessons as a way to enhance their appreciation of higher culture.
4. Supported her children in overcoming academic obstacles by encouraging them 'to go the extra mile' and never give up.
5. Emphasized the prestige of being a professional such as a medical doctor, a teacher, or a lawyer.
6. Fostered a love for reading.
7. Supported her children's studies with the family's scarce resources.
8. Celebrated her children's efforts and successes at school by preparing their favorite dishes as a reward.
9. Became literate at age 51 and finished high school when she turned 81.

Thanks to my mother, I was able to:

a) learn English as a second language in Cuba shortly after turning 16;
b) work as a stenographer when I was 16;
c) become the first member of the family to enter and finish college – the unique circumstances of my university education are recounted in *Havana-Mérida-Chicago*;
d) become a college instructor six months before finishing my bachelor's degree;

e) attain a master's degree in Great Britain, having been sent there because I was the only faculty member in the Operational Research Department of the College of Economics at the University of Havana with a mastery of English;

f) attain two doctoral degrees in economics from the Ukrainian Academy of Sciences.

My mother instilled in me a passion for learning and the satisfaction of getting good grades for the sake of learning rather than for material benefits that were, in fact, only attainable after leaving Cuba for good. She is responsible for my love of the teaching vocation, the pleasure of transmitting knowledge in a comprehensible way to my students and of developing their reasoning skills, as well as the commitment I have to excellence. All of these factors led to me receiving the highest award I could ever dream of – the 2007 Excellence in Teaching Award from DePaul University, the college of my dreams where I had been working as an adjunct instructor of Economics for 12 years and as an Invited Assistant Professor of International Studies for another seven years. I simply do not have the words to express the gratitude I owe my mother. She still lives on in my beloved teaching.

My mother's example goes beyond the impact she had on me. She touched the lives of many young people while studying in high school in her 70s. She encouraged them to continue with their education and to meet obstacles. Through this book and its effect on my readers, I also see that she is leaving a legacy. Being illiterate did not keep her from being a role model in the education of her family.

Moreover, she is telling all the parents reading this book that limited education must not keep them from becoming role models in the education of their children. It is up to the parents to use the power that the Lord placed in their hands when they brought their children into the world.

Before residing in this country, I always used two last names: Morales from my father and Pita from my mother. When I immigrated to the U.S. for good, I learned that using the two last names might create confusion since Americans only use their father's last name. My spiritual father, Reverend Edgar Morales, informed me that I could only use my mother's last name if I used it with a hyphen. So on my social-security card, the name written is Antonio E. Morales-Pita. Therefore, even though I could not attend my mother's funeral in Cuba for political reasons, she permanently remains a part of me in my last name and, of course, in my heart.

**Food for Thought**

Invitation to meditate:

In the context of becoming a role model for the readers' children, please, think:

1. Be it for economic, educational level, age-related or social reasons, are the readers willing and/or able to assume this important responsibility?
2. Is there any unsurmountable obstacle for excluding yourself from helping your children in this role?

# Chapter V
## How to Inspire Anybody to Overcome a Challenge?

*"There is one quality that one must possess to win, and that is definiteness of purpose, the knowledge of what one wants and a burning desire to possess it."*

– Napoleon Hill,
popular author of books on personal achievement and success

Since this book does not pretend to inform the reader how to inspire anybody in every specific context, you may ask, "Wouldn't it be wonderful if this book could help inspire my partner to be more cooperative and evenly share all the chores at home?" Or, "If I am facing a crisis such as coping with the aftermath of a heart attack and need to find an inspirational person to restore my spirit, wouldn't it be fantastic if the book could help me identify that person?"

Since life is so rich and full of challenges, it is more useful if I give the reader general instruments to cope with whatever challenge he or she is confronting.

You can see from Chapter III that as an educator, I try to foster in my students reasoning skills instead of rote memorization. Let me give you an example of the different outcomes that result from instilling in students these different skill sets.

Somebody once told me the story of a man who wanted a fish to eat but did not have enough money to buy one at the market, so he approached a fisherman holding a basket full of fish. The man asked the fisherman for a part of his catch. If the fisherman handed him a fish, the man would have happily gone home and satisfied his immediate hunger. Sometime later, however, this man would be hungry again and in the same situation. If the fisherman refused to give the man what he was asking for and instead taught him how to fish, the man would have solved the problem of getting fish once and for all. This book attempts to teach the reader how to be inspirational and how to be inspired in any circumstance. After developing theoretical approaches in Chapters I and II, it provides examples of situations in the classroom, and at home.

Looking at my own personal experience and the inspirational books I have come across, I can summarize the three conditions that are necessary and sufficient to overcome a challenge through inspirational means. These conditions are having a problem that needs to be solved (in other words, a motivation to act), having the courage to 'take the bull by the horns,' and finding the means to resolve the problem.

A sane person needs to be motivated to solve a problem. This motivation may come from within or may be produced by an inspiration from an outside source. Without the specific need to act, the subject of our general story would not require inspiration. So, the first step toward solving a problem or taking a given course of action is to find the motivation to face the challenge. The second step is to identify the source of motivation, be it internal or external to the person. The third step is to concentrate on the objective and develop the tenacity to follow up after the initial push, sticking with the objective through thick and thin. For the tenacious person, there will always be a justification to undertake action; for the volatile person who changes direction and is unsure of the course of action that should be taken, there is always an excuse.

In my course, Introduction to Macroeconomics, which I just taught during the second summer quarter of 2010 at DePaul University, I met a tenacious student whose story exemplifies the aforementioned process. She did not have solid mathematical skills and was struggling with the graphs and the mathematical procedures required to get through the course.

Her score on the midterm exam was low. She was frustrated but wanted to continue in the class and did not give up.

- Step 1 – She had the motivation to learn macroeconomics because it was a requirement of her major and she would need to understand it in her future professional career. She paid for the course out of her own pocket and knew that she was learning. Her objective was not only to pass; she also needed to learn the subject.

- Step 2 – She had to study harder, but she needed outside help. She asked me and one of her peers to help her, and she studied very hard. She found the motivation internally as well as externally from her instructor and peer.
- Step 3 – She concentrated on the objective and mustered all her tenacity to study and learn. She punctually attended class sessions, studied every day until reaching the point of exhaustion. The night before the exam, following my advice, she rested. She got a terrific score on the final exam and achieved a very good grade in the course.

Over my 55-year career, I have found students who struggled with the same subject matter but were not tenacious. Their only motivation was to pass, not to learn. They needed to pass the course to meet their curriculum requirements, not because they were aware of the importance of the course to their professional career. In reality, they needed a degree to make more money. Their attendance was not perfect. Their punctuality was sporadic even though they were penalized for tardiness. They were not inspired by my passion for teaching. They were always looking for excuses, blaming somebody else for their own mistakes, and asking that they be exempted from the requirements of the syllabus. There was always a reason beyond their reach for not delivering the assignments on time. Their computers would crash, and they did not have the time to get to the university to use the computers there. They suddenly got a terrible headache and the pills did not work. This type of student may or may not pass, but if they do, they will forget the things they crammed into their minds at the same speed as quickly procrastinating attitudes allowed them to fall behind.

Many people draw up a list of personal resolutions at the beginning of a new year. Some of them stick to their goals. Others start at the beginning of January, but after a while, they get discouraged and discontinue because of some excuse or another (in reality, they did not have enough tenacity to keep on and overcome the obstacles that life presented them). So, tenacity plays an important role in overcoming obstacles even after one has been inspired.

Not everybody is tenacious, and very few people have the tenacity to continue in every undertaking. But everybody can demonstrate tenacity if need be, at least to a degree. Sometimes the need to be tenacious is so great that even the most reluctant and apathetic person is moved to find motivation. Bear in mind that the motivation to overcome a challenge is only the first step. Find it inside yourself. If you believe in God, pray relentlessly for help. If you are not a believer, find the strength inside yourself. The option is yours.

This book would not be complete if it did not include a real example of the impact of inspiration from the perspective of an inspired person. Life has given me the opportunity to witness many examples, like that of Puerto Rican, the mother studying macroeconomics at St. Augustine College while one of her children was suffering a terminal condition. The child stayed at the hospital for months, but my student maintained perfect attendance. Oftentimes she would receive a call that her son was having a crisis, and she would go to the hospital once more to be beside him, but she would always return the following week. She passed the course satisfactorily, and she graduated. At the commencement ceremony, she was accompanied by all her children. When I congratulated her for getting her associate degree in accounting, I asked, "Are you going to be promoted at work after obtaining this degree?" She stared at me as only a mother can do and answered, pointing to her children, including one who was sitting in a wheelchair, "Yes, I will move ahead from being a receptionist to an accountant assistant, but the main reason I finished the degree is to set an example for them. If their mother could finish her degree when Manolo was in the hospital for months, waiting for a transplant, they can also finish their studies, go to college, and graduate as their mother did. This was my motivation to try so hard."

It is also time to include the experience of one of the students who was impacted by inspiration, Mr. Evans, (whose name has been changed because I could not contact the person) who has co-written the last chapter of this book with me.

I know that you are anxious to read Mr. Evan's testimony, but, first, it would be wise for you to meditate:

**Food for Thought**
Invitation to meditate:

1. Do you remember to have overcome an important obstacle in your life? If so, why or how could you do it?

2.  Have you ever felt unable to get over an important barrier or impediment? If so, why or how couldn't you?

In each case, the readers are asked to analyze the motivation and the sources of inspiration that were required to overcome the challenge. The most useful part of these questions is that the readers are asked to analyze why one of the outcomes was successful and the other was not. Thereby, they should discover the reasons for the different results. This is a way to develop readers' analytic and cognitive skills in order to enhance their inspirational ability.

# Chapter VI

# A Groundbreaking
# Inspirational Story

*"Develop a passion for learning. If you do, you will never cease to grow."*

– Anthony J. D'Angelo,
personal development guru and leader in student/faculty empowerment.

I have always been an advocate of putting theory into practice in order to verify the conclusions of a given body of scientific work. After presenting my own theory about inspiration and its effect on human beings, and also as the finale to this book, I would like to provide a living example of the inspirational process between an inspiring educator and an inspired student.

It was back in the spring quarter of the 2009-2010 academic year at DePaul University. I was teaching two sections of INT-150 (Global Connections) and one section of Focal Point about Karl Marx. The awesome experience that I am about to relate began in the morning session of INT-150.

This course is an elective. Students from all majors, as well as students who have not yet picked a major, can enroll in the course. The course has the distinctive characteristic of being taught very differently, depending on who the instructor is. If the instructor is a sociologist, he or she will emphasize the social aspects of globalization. If he or she happens to be a political scientist, the political dimension of globalization will be emphasized. I am an economist, and therefore my focus in the course was international political economy.

Each time I teach this course, I find that the enrollment comprises quite a variety of students ranging from freshmen to seniors with majors as diverse as economics, chemistry, music, and biology. I have met excellent students and not so excellent ones, hardworking students with excellent attendance and a commitment to learning, and students who try to pass with minimal effort. The wide variety of academic interests of the students usually makes teaching the course extremely interesting.

One of the students in the aforementioned section was going to have an unforgettable effect on my teaching career and is an example of the mutual inspirational process between an educator and a student.

Mr. Evans was a very committed student with a record of impeccable attendance and eager participation in the class. He was always ready to answer hard questions, which showed that he had understood the subject. He formulated questions, the answers to which went well beyond the scope of the class. He was articulate and quick-witted in his answers.

The best part of the course is a research project that the students develop in the last two or three weeks. The students are supposed to make an oral presentation in PowerPoint and deliver a written report.

Mr. Evans did a solid piece of research about China's socio-economic and political situation and the interdependence between the Chinese and the U.S. economies. When he was making his oral presentation, I was flabbergasted, stunned, and sort of mesmerized. He was speaking by taking the PowerPoint presentation as a guide, but explaining the tables and charts with a mastery, corresponding to that of a graduate student. He did not do any reading in his delivery. He knew the subject matter so well that he was able to talk about it without referring to any notecards. I didn't have to ask him any questions. Everything was so clearly explained that it was evident he had an in-depth knowledge of his subject and explained it with a sharp, pedagogical focus. I had to contain myself from exclaiming: Bravo! Impeccable! Flawless! I had to consider that the remaining students would feel diminished by my expressions, because their presentations had not inspired me in the same way. I said (as modestly as I could) that his presentation was outstanding. I shook his hand and congratulated him. His presentation took up the last part of the class, and I went to my office immediately afterward.

I sat down in my chair and felt happiness within myself. I had witnessed the miracle of what inspiration could produce in a student. He showed a deep commitment to research and was the living promise of a future scientist. I had to talk to him about doing a joint paper about the topic on which he had given the presentation. Coincidentally, I knew of an international seminar being held in Pittsburgh in September, 2009. The professor in charge of the event had invited me to present a paper about international political economy, and I thought this student's presentation, further developed through additional research, could well be that presentation. The paper was chosen for inclusion in the conference which we both attended. I wanted him to present two-thirds of the paper, and I delivered the conclusion. When questions were asked by the highly expert audience (all whom held doctoral degrees), I preferred that he answer with only minimal participation on my part. I had the pleasure of witnessing how my inspired student was able to answer questions with the certitude and maturity of a seasoned economist. If he was nervous on the inside, he was adult enough to control himself and not reveal it. I felt very inspired to see my inspired student. The success story goes on, but I prefer that Sydney tell it himself. I have explained my side of the inspirational story. Now it is his turn to describe the process of being inspired as a student.

## Mr. Evans's Contribution to the Book

My name is Mr. Sidney Evans. "As I sit in a hotel room in Beijing, I have been asked by my great friend, Dr. Morales-Pita, to recount the events in my life that have led me to this faraway land.

It is a story that began in a small classroom of only a few students on the Lincoln Park campus of DePaul University in the spring 2009 quarter. This was my last quarter before getting my Bachelor of Arts in Political Science.

As a graduating senior with plans to attend law school, I had signed up for a basic-level international studies class with a professor with whom I was unfamiliar. I still remember the feeling of unexpected excitement when a well-dressed Latin-American gentleman entered the room with the enthusiasm of a young boy at Christmas time. He began explaining that the class would focus on the issue of globalization in the context of international political economy.

I immediately wondered why exactly this gentleman was so excited about the process of globalization. As the class session went on, Dr. Morales-Pita told the class the story of his life living in five countries. Then I could answer my question. This gentleman epitomizes what it is to live in a globalized society: a man from Cuba, who spent time as a teenage tourist in the United States, who did his master's degree in Scotland and two doctorates in Ukraine, who worked as a professor and a leader of a multidisciplinary research team in two Mexican universities, and who finally ended up in Chicago, teaching classes in economics and international studies. In my opinion, this is the personalization of the true meaning of globalization.

I remember leaving class that day with two feelings: firstly, I could learn a great deal from a man with this sort of diverse experience; secondly, I was left with the feeling that he had worked so hard to achieve all he had during his lifetime that I could never let my work disappoint him. At the time, I was unsure what caused my need for approval from Dr. Morales-Pita. I realize now that Dr. Morales-Pita – on the first day of class through his energy, knowledge of the subject, pedagogical methodology, and life story – had planted the seeds of inspiration inside me. During the next few weeks, this professor watered these seeds by relaying his knowledge of the diverse economic occurrences across the globe.

Some weeks later, Dr. Morales-Pita assigned topics for a presentation and a paper that would be due at the end of the quarter. I remember the following moment as if it were yesterday. He suggested China for my paper topic. The way he looked at me with the suggestion stuck with me for years. His persuasion conveyed a confidence and excitement about the work I would produce regarding my topic.

When the class session was over, I went running home with such excitement. I couldn't wait to arrive at my computer and begin researching Chinese economics. All it took to inspire me on this day was the look Dr. Morales-Pita gave me, which showed his faith in my abilities. China is a very complex country mixing a communist political direction with the introduction of the market economy. He thought I could do it, and I could not disappoint him.

During the process of writing this paper, I would stop by Dr. Morales-Pita's office regularly to ask questions about the materials I was finding and their relevance to my paper. I believe during these discussions that he saw in me an ability to be inspired. I remember him asking me one day, "What are your plans post-graduation?" I told Dr. Morales about my plans for law school. He was sort of surprised by my answer and said, "I think you can become a good lawyer, although you could have a great future as a political economist." That was all I needed. With Dr. Morales's help, I learned to love research, and I knew that law school did not offer me this same joy. At this time, I knew I had to prove to my mentor through my presentation that his feeling was justified and that I could succeed in the field of economics.

I was nervous on the day of the presentation because I felt this unquenchable need to show Dr. Morales that his faith in me had not been unfounded. I gave my presentation and was pleased with how it went. Dr. Morales told me I had done a fantastic job. From that moment onward, I no longer looked forward to law school. I was convinced economics was the path that my future must take. After our last class, my professor told me to stay behind for some minutes because he wanted to discuss something with me. This was the meeting that changed my life.

Dr. Morales sat me down and said, "Mr. Evans, it would be a loss to the economic community if you did not pursue further studies in this field. I would like to take your paper as a model and combine our efforts to create a paper for publication in an academic journal." This was all I needed to hear. Dr. Morales had inspired me in a way I had never been before. When I arrived home that evening, I called my father to tell him that I would forego plans to attend law school. I wanted to stay at DePaul University and take an extra year in order to pursue a graduate degree in economics.

Over the next several months, I spent many hours in Dr. Morales's office working on our new paper and discussing the process of preparing for graduate education. He exhausted all of his contacts, setting up meetings with various economics professors so they could lend advice to me on achieving my new goal.

All the while, through Dr. Morales's tutelage, we formulated a paper. He fostered a love of research inside of me. He showed me how taking data and interpreting results can be an unbelievably rewarding practice.

While we created a paper, I started to realize that my mentor was creating something much greater. He was creating a man with the skills required not only to succeed in economic research but in all walks of life. On several occasions, we would take breaks from writing, and he would tell me a story from his life. These stories were not only interesting, but they also possessed the secrets to having a life full of love, happiness, and contentment. I can safely say that I grew more as a person during these meetings than I had during my entire time attending college.

One day, Dr. Morales came to me with an opportunity to present the paper we had been crafting at an economic conference in Pittsburgh. He said that – if the paper goes well at this conference – we would most likely find a publisher of an academic journal to publish our work. Our paper was complete, and we were both ready to present it to the world.

In September, 2009, as we arrived in Pittsburgh, I was unsure what to expect from this conference. Dr. Morales quenched my fears with stories of his dissertations and the hardship he had undergone to complete this process in the Soviet Union. Through these stories, Dr. Morales gave me the feeling that, with his help, any task could be completed. I realize now he was also raising my confidence in my own work, so when the day came, he could set me free and allow my skills to fly.

During the conference, my mentor treated me like an equal in a room full of Ph.D. professors from different universities; he exuded a confidence that made me feel I belonged in that habitat. This confidence transferred over to our presentation. It went fantastically. As a result, our paper was published in an international electronic journal in Poland after being approved by a board of specialists.

Many people may think this was the end of Dr. Morales's mentoring: taking an undergraduate student looking for direction to a graduate student who had accomplished a goal which most undergraduates could not even dream of accomplishing. I am thankful to say this was not even close to the end. As I completed the school year, Dr. Morales and I had very regular meeting to discuss the future of my education. He offered help and advice while showing his confidence that I would make the correct decision because of the skills he had instilled in me. I realized shortly into the application process for graduate school that I needed to take a page from the book of the man who had given me so much love and guidance by earning my master's degree abroad. Where else would I study but the country that had started this great journey: China!

As I prepared to leave for China, I remembered very distinctly the last meeting I had with Dr. Morales. I remember the look in his eyes, which was similar to the one when he suggested me doing the presentation on China. The same confidence and excitement were present in his face, but now there was a new emotion. It was pride, not only for what I had achieved during the time he had mentored me but also in his ability to help mold a student into a professional that could walk in any circle, compete intellectually with any person, and possess a joy that is truly rare. He had kept the training wheels on his student, and it was time to let him fly with the skills he had instilled in him.

This brings me back to my hotel room in Beijing; it would be a lie to tell the reader that the recounting of this story did not bring many tears to my face. These are tears of joy. Having the perspective to look back on my time with Dr. Morales, I know now that before going to class every day, he thinks of how best to convey – his lecture – to the class in order to instill in his students the passion and love for the subject matter to be taught. I am very confident – though – that he had no idea he could change the trajectory of a life forever. After I complete my time here in Beijing, I will return to Chicago, not only because it is a city I have fallen in love with but also because I know that I have a friend waiting there for me with plans of changing another student's life for the better. Taking my experience as a point of reference, he will probably accomplish his goal. This is the sign of a great man who starts every day with the goal of inspiring at least one person."

This story is an example of what can be done under the impact of an inspiration. If you discover the need to be inspired, go back to this experience, go back to this book, reread the different sections, and you will also be inspired. If you meet somebody facing a challenge and in need of help, try to find in your inner self the inspirational part of your personality, something at which you are really good, and put it to work. Inspire anyone! The reward is enormous! GOOD LUCK!

It is a wonderful feeling to know that you are able to inspire someone to change his or her life for the better. It is a rewarding feeling to be inspired by some inspirational person and to receive the benefits of the inspiration. Attempt to inspire anyone and attempt to be inspired by that special person or source of inspiration that you admire. May the Lord allow this book to become a friend to be consulted and to be inspired from! After thoroughly reading the book, you have the tools to work and the procedures to follow. Now it is all up to you. Once more, I need to wish you GOOD LUCK! It would be wonderful to receive your comments. My email address: amoralespita1@gmail.com is waiting for your feedback.

**Food for Thought**

Deeply meditate about this question. Being passionate and tenacious will help an individual to be inspired (or to be inspired) for a long time and allow him/her to overcome a hurdle?